COWS of OUR PLANET

A Far Side
collection

Other Books in The Far Side Series

The Far Side
Beyond The Far Side
In Search of The Far Side
Bride of The Far Side
Valley of The Far Side
It Came From The Far Side
Hound of The Far Side
The Far Side Observer
Night of the Crash-Test Dummies
Wildlife Preserves
Wiener Dog Art
Unnatural Selections

Anthologies

The Far Side Gallery
The Far Side Gallery 2
The Far Side Gallery 3

Retrospective

The PreHistory of The Far Side: A 10th Anniversary Exhibit

COWS of OUR PLANET

A Far Side
collection
by
Gary Larson

Andrews and McMeel
A Universal Press Syndicate Company
Kansas City

ISBN: 0-8362-1701-2
Library of Congress Catalog Card Number: 92-72254

"Hey . . . this could be the chief."

While their owners sleep, nervous
little dogs prepare for their day.

Colonel Sanders at the Pearly Gates

Three more careers are claimed by
the Bermuda Triangle of jazz.

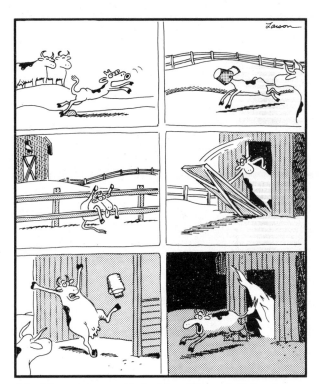

The life and times of Lulu, Mrs. O'Leary's ill-fated cow

7

Basic lives

The herd moved in around him, but Zach had known better than to approach these animals without his trusty buffalo gum.

"Margaret! You? . . . I . . . I . . . should . . . have . . . knowwwwwwnnnnn . . ."

Unbeknownst to most ornithologists, the dodo was actually a very advanced species, living alone quite peacefully until, in the 17th century, it was annihilated by men, rats, and dogs. As usual.

Unwittingly, Raymond wanders into the hive's company picnic.

And then Al realized his problems were much
bigger than just a smashed truck.

"Look. We know *how* you did it — *how* is no longer
the question. What we now want to know is
why. . . . Why now, brown cow?"

"I tell ya, Ben — no matter who wins this thing,
Boot Hill ain't ever gonna be the same."

"OK, McFadden. . . . So *that's* the way you wanna play."

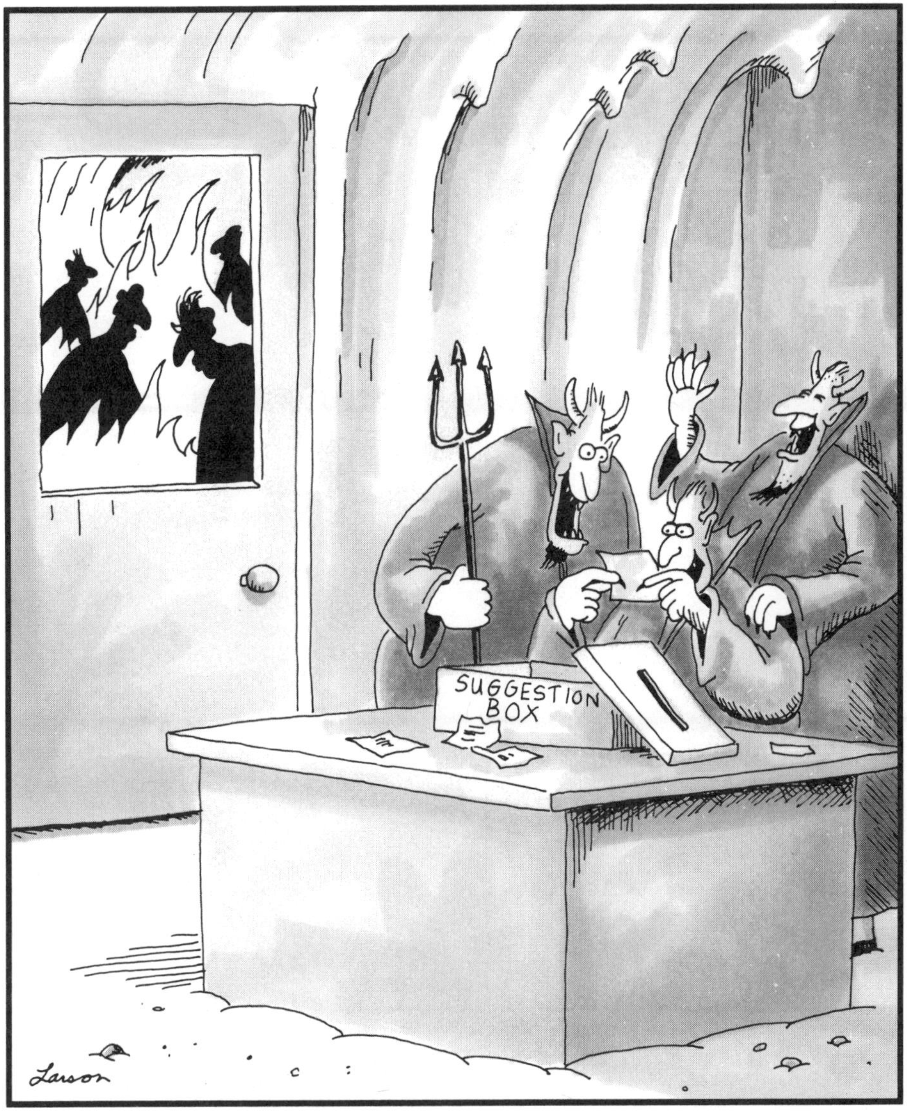
SUGGESTION BOX

Every afternoon a sugar cube dealer would slowly cruise the corral looking for "customers."

Modern art critic

"Man, the Kellermans are bold! . . . If it wasn't for our screens, they'd probably walk right in!"

How to recognize the moods of an Irish setter

"Well, first the bad news — you're definitely hooked."

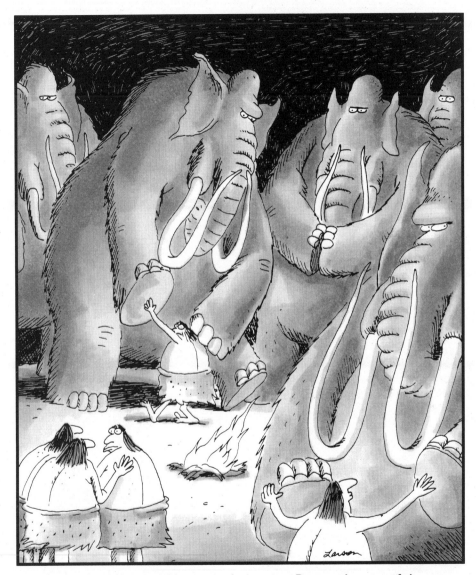

Tomorrow, they would be mortal enemies. But on the eve of the great hunt, feelings were put aside for the traditional Mammoth Dance.

The action suddenly stopped while both sides waited
patiently for the hornet to calm down.

Eventually, Billy came to dread his father's lectures over all other forms of punishment.

On the air with "Snake Talk"

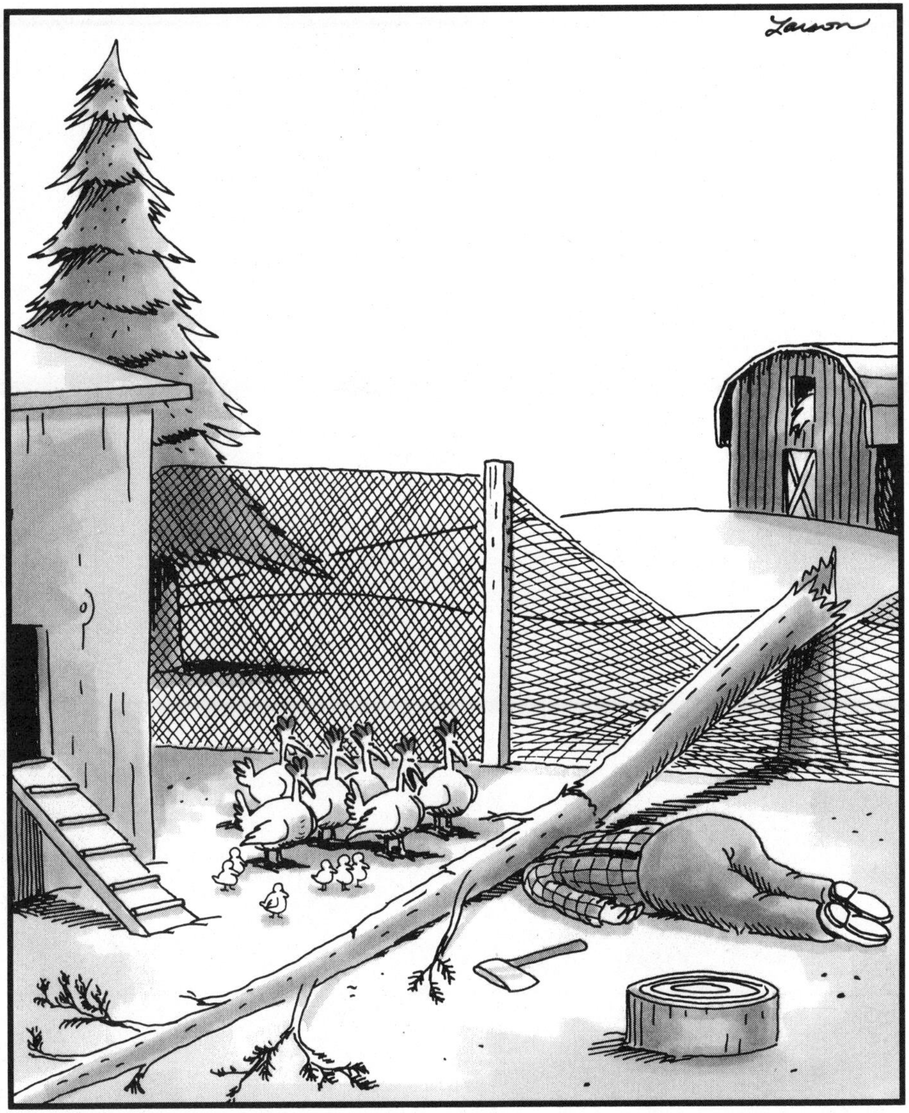
Larson

"Lord, we thank thee."

Vera looked around the room. Not another chicken anywhere. And then it struck her — this was a hay bar.

Junior high gorillas

For many weeks, the two species had lived in mutual tolerance of one another. And then, without provocation, the hornets began throwing rocks at Ned's house.

Abraham Lincoln's first car

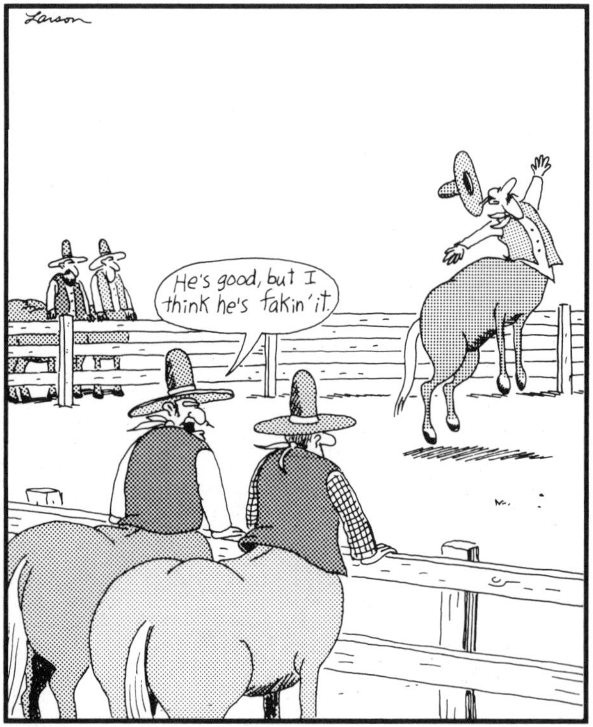
Larson
He's good, but I think he's fakin' it.

Centaur rodeos

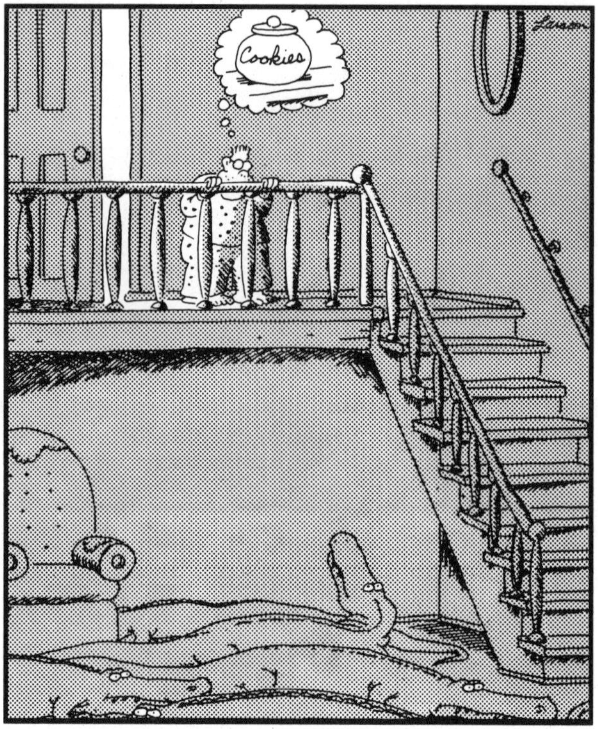
Larson
Cookies

The nightly crisis of Todd's stomach vs.
Todd's imagination

How poodles first came to North America

Suddenly, Fish and Wildlife agents burst in on
Mark Trail's poaching operation.

The first Dirt Capades

The life and times of baby Jessica

"Look here, McGinnis — hundreds of bright copper kettles, warm woolen mittens, brown paper packages tied up with string. . . . Someone was after a few of this guy's favorite things."

High above the hushed crowd, Rex tried to remain
focused. Still, he couldn't shake one nagging thought:
He was an old dog and this was a new trick.

Hell's video store

Custer's recurrent nightmare

"Same as the others, O'Neill. The flippers, the
fishbowl, the frog, the lights, the armor. . . .
Just one question remains: Is this the work
of our guy, or a copycat?"

Sumo temporaries

"Well, there he goes again. . . . I suppose I shouldn't
worry, but I just get a bad feeling about
Jimmy hanging with those tuna punks."

Fortunately for Sparky, Zeke knew the
famous "Rex maneuver."

Henry never knew what hit him.

"And so please welcome one of this cartoon's most esteemed scientist-like characters, Professor Boris Needleman, here to present his paper, 'Beyond the Border: Analysis, Statistical Probability, and Speculation of the Existence of Other Cartoons on the Known Comics Page.'"

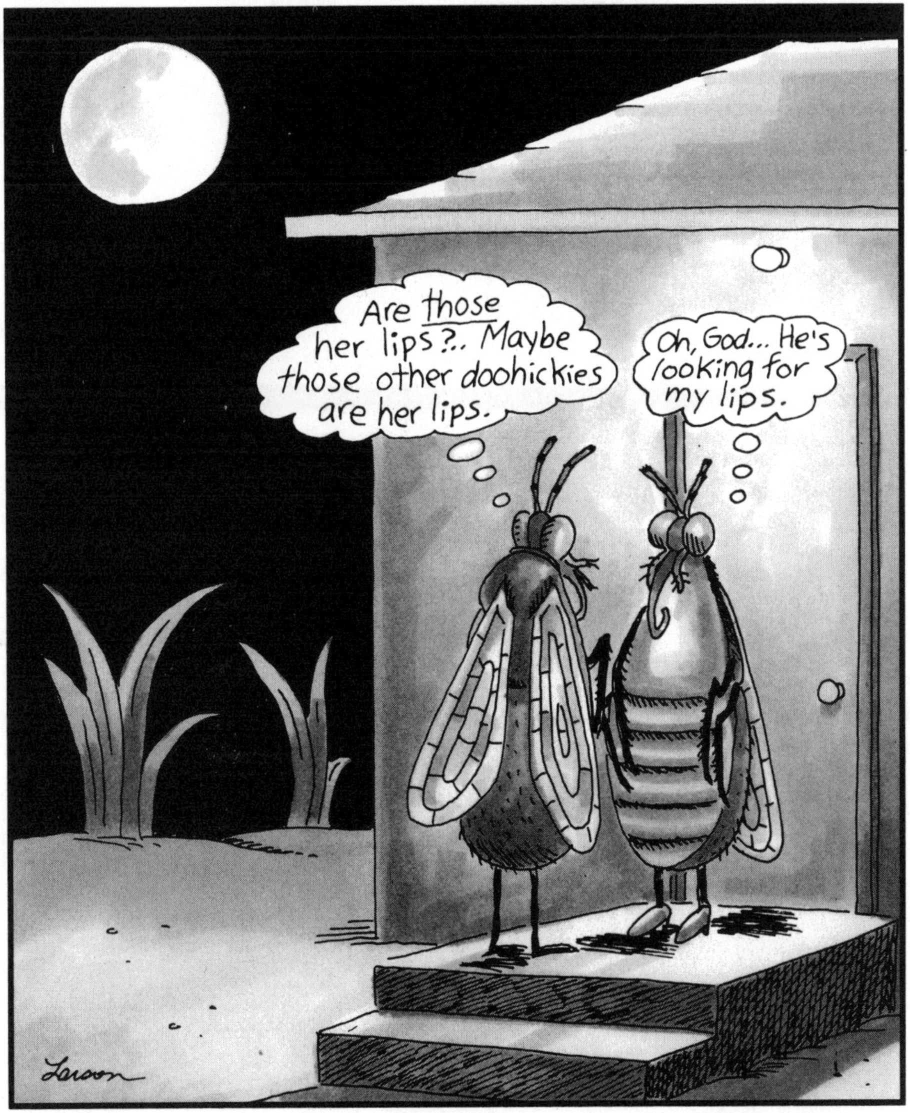
Are those her lips?.. Maybe those other doohickies are her lips.
Oh, God... He's looking for my lips.
Larson

Fly dates

"Well, we're ready for the males' 100-meter freestyle, and I think we can rest assured that most of these athletes will select the dog paddle."

At the monthly meeting of Squidheads Anonymous

35

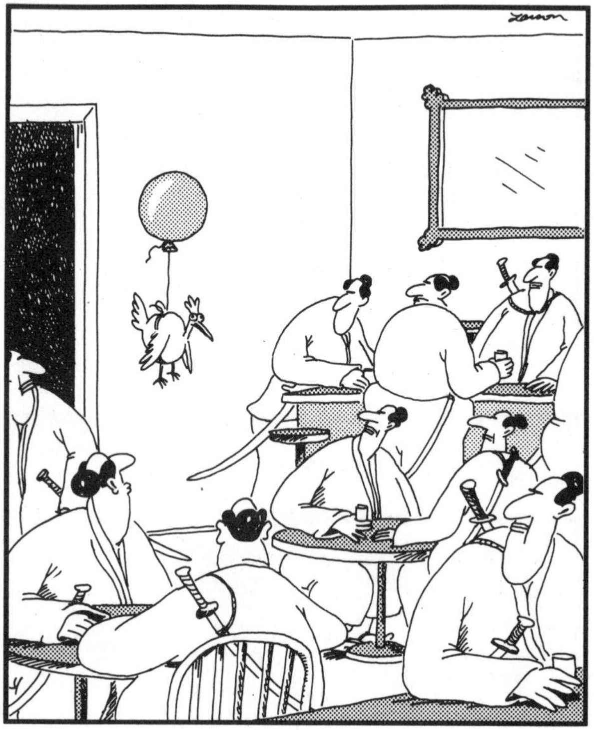

In what was destined to be a short-lived spectacle, a chicken, suspended by a balloon, floated through the Samurai bar's doorway.

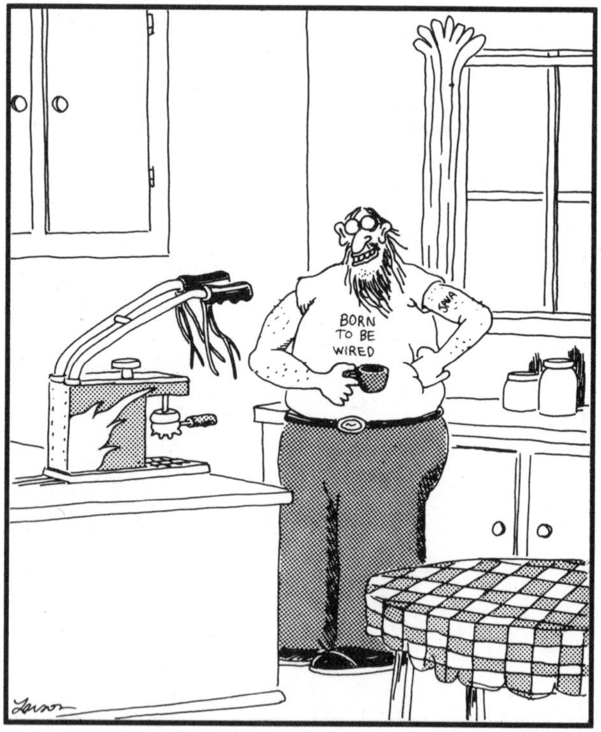
BORN
TO BE
WIRED
JAVA

Carl "Javahead" Jones and his chopped espresso maker

"Curse you, Flannegan! Curse you to *hell*! . . . there, I've said it."

"Voila! . . . Your new dream home! If you like it,
I can get a crew mixing wood fibers and saliva
as early as tomorrow."

"Oh, my God, Rogers! . . . Is that? . . . Is that?
It is! It's the *mummy's purse!*"

"According to these figures, Simmons, your department has lost another No. 2 Double A, and I want you to find it!"

"Give me a hand here, boys! It's young Will Hawkins! . . . Dang fool tried to ride into the sunset!"

"You gotta help me, Mom. . . . This assignment is due tomorrow, and Gramps doesn't understand the new tricks."

Charlie Brown in Indian country

Carl had never had so much fun in his whole life, and he knew, from this moment on, that he would never again be a lone pine tree.

Professor Glickman, the lab practical joker, deftly
places a single drop of hydrochloric acid on
the back of Professor Bingham's neck.

Mike Wallace interviews the Devil.

That night, their revenge was meted out on both Farmer O'Malley and his wife. The next day, police investigators found a scene that they could describe only as "grisly, yet strangely hilarious."

Social morays

Stumpy didn't know how he got in this situation,
but with the whole town watching, he knew
he'd have to play it out.

Roommates Elvis and Salman Rushdie sneak a
quick look at the outside world.

Donning his new canine decoder, Professor Schwartzman becomes the first human being on Earth to hear what barking dogs are actually saying.

"You're a long way from Big Poodle, stranger. . . .
This here is Dead Skunk, and if I were you
I'd just keep on movin'."

"Why don't you play some blues, Andrew?"

"New guy, huh? Well, up here, you walk the *edge*! And the edge is a fickle hellcat. . . . Love her, but never trust her, for her heart is full of *lye*!"

God at His computer

By blending in with the ostrich's eggs, Hare Krishnas are subsequently raised by the adult birds.

Punk worms

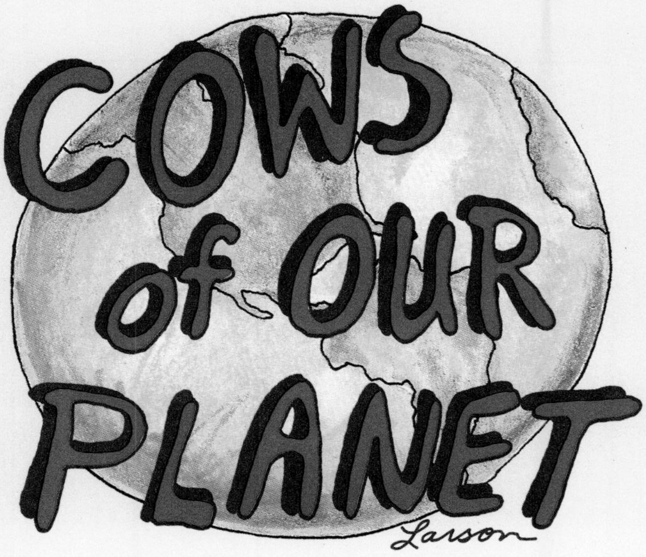
COWS of OUR PLANET
Larson

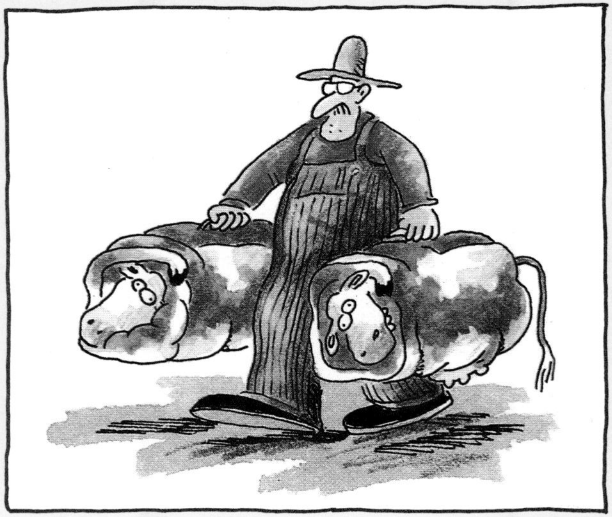

New Zealand portaford

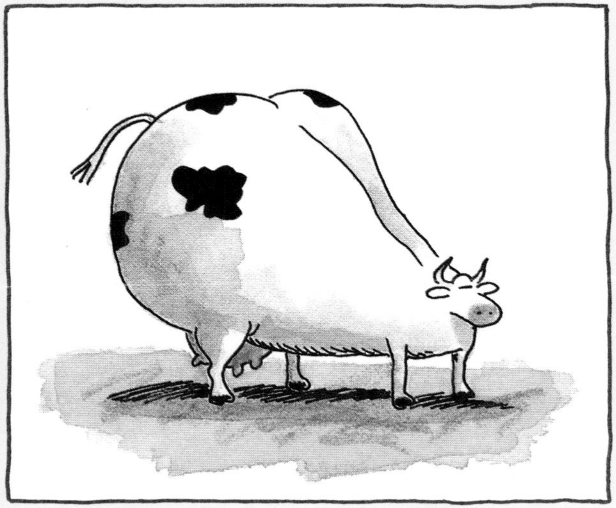

Tennessee big butt

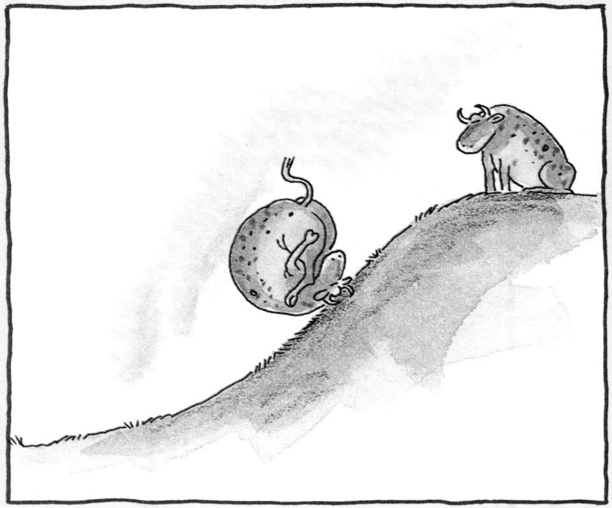

Australian spotted roller

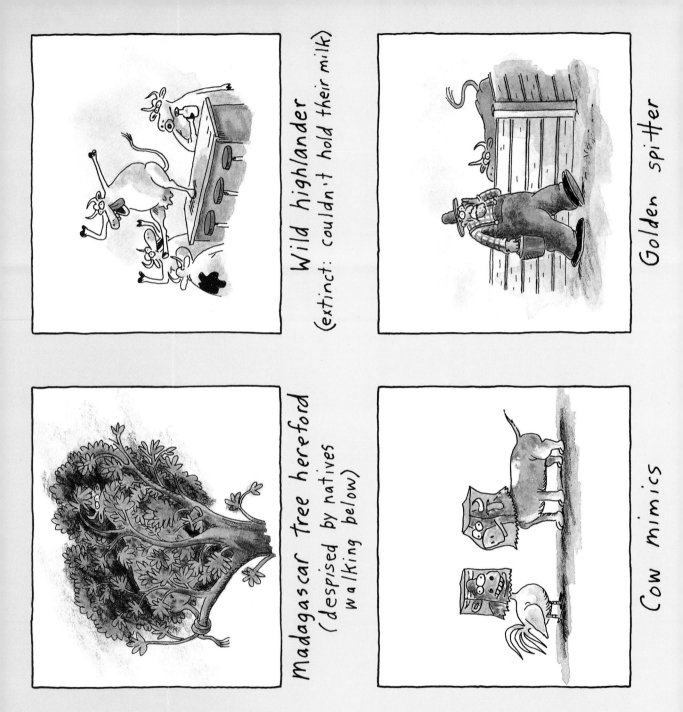

Wild highlander
(extinct: couldn't hold their milk)

Golden spitter

Madagascar tree hereford
(despised by natives
walking below)

Cow mimics

Urban street hereford
(rarely seen)

Western skipper

Three Mile Island guernsey
(North American cousin to
the Chernobyl angus)

Amazon river cow

Norwegian one-eyed smiler

Flying guernsey

Skyscraper suckerfoot

close-up of hoof

Brahma belly

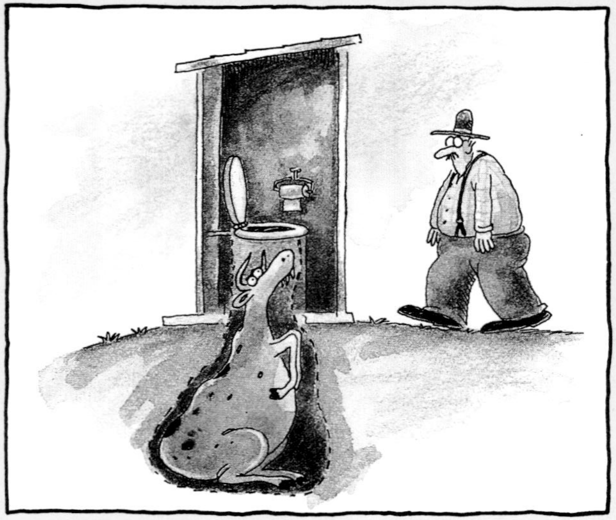

Idaho latrine stalker
(venomous)

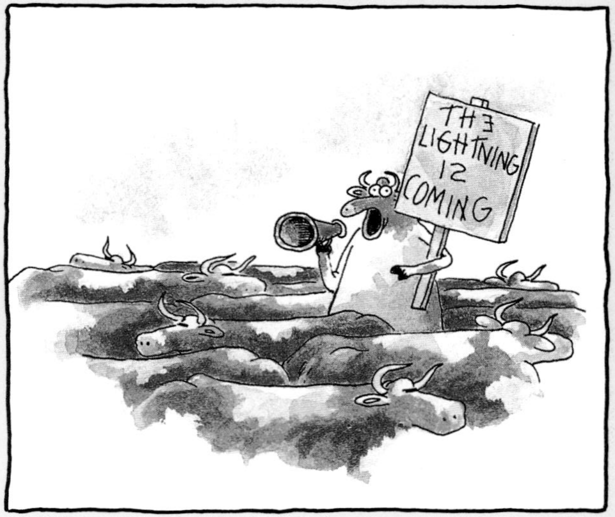
THE LIGHTNING IZ COMING

Blue-faced stampede agitator
(usually shot by ranchers)

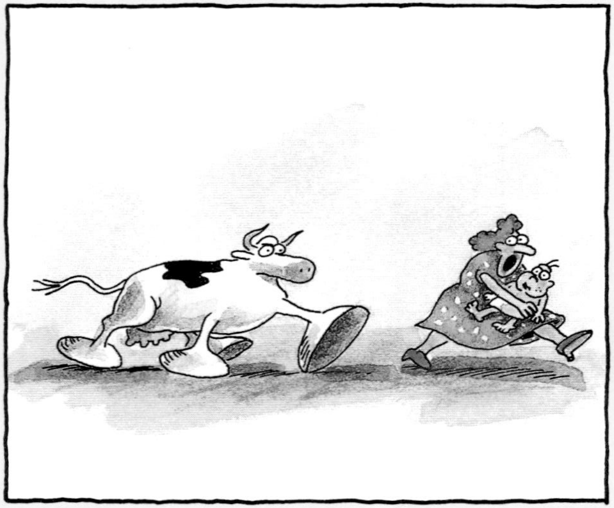

Arkansas baby stomper

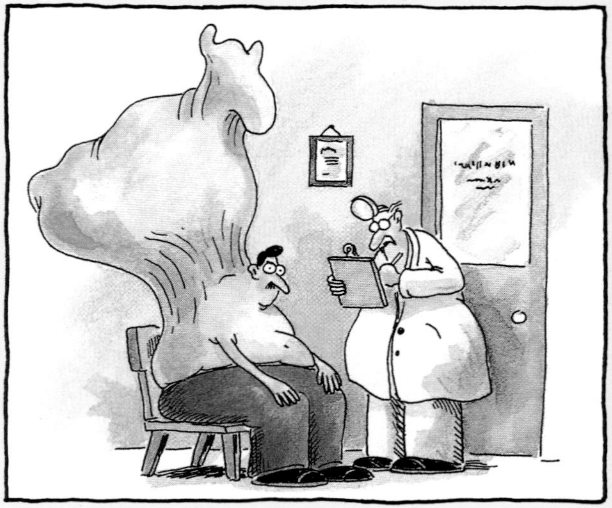

Parasitic charolais

Polynesian puffer cow

Before   After

Mad scientist hybrid
(happened only once, in the '50s)

BOB'S
SLAUGHTERHOUSE

Help me!
Help me!

Texas longnose
(recently extinct: certain cultures
thought the nose was an aphrodisiac)

Toy angus
(extinct)

"Bad guy comin' in, Arnie! . . . Minor key!"

"Whoa! Mr. Lewis! We don't know what that thing is or where it came from, but after what happened to the dog last week, we advise people not to touch it."

Special commuter lanes

"Yeah, Vern! You heard what I said! And what are you gonna do about it? Huh? C'mon! What are ya gonna do? Huh? *C'mon!*"

Dog ventriloquists

"Hey! I got news for you, sweetheart! . . .
I *am* the lowest form of life on earth!"

The art of conversation

Sheep that pass in the night

"Whoa! Whoa! C'mon, you guys! This is just a friendly game of cards — ease up on those acid-filled beakers."

"I hate 'em. They mess on the stools, they attack the mirror — and, of course, they drink like birds."

Of course, prehistoric neighborhoods always had that one family whose front yard was strewn with old mammoth remains.

". . . And please let Mom, Dad, Rex, Ginger, Tucker, me, and all the rest of the family see color."

Cornered and sensing danger,
Sidney flares his "eye spots."

"Oooooo! Check it out, Edith! It's a *quadra*ceratops!"

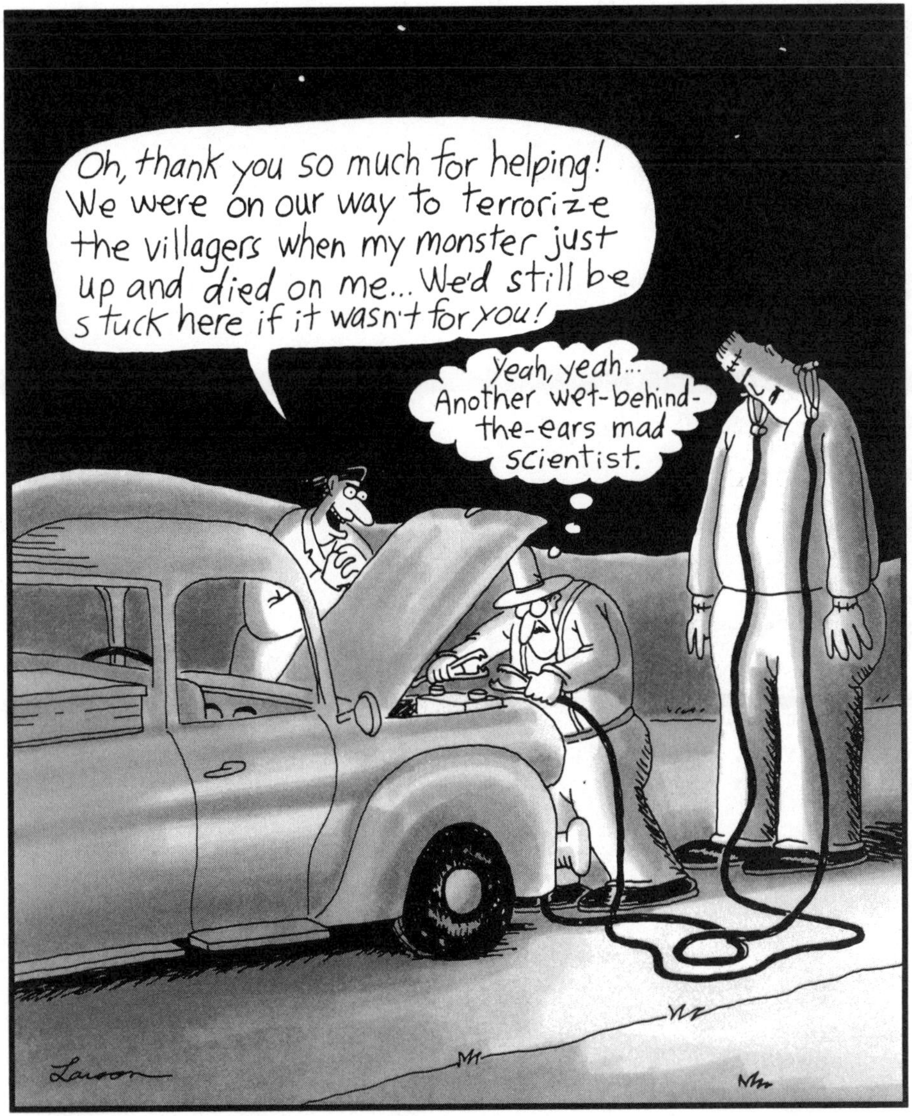
Oh, thank you so much for helping! We were on our way to terrorize the villagers when my monster just up and died on me... We'd still be stuck here if it wasn't for *you!*
Yeah, yeah... Another wet-behind-the-ears mad scientist.
Larson

"I wouldn't do that, bartender. . . . Unless, of course,
you think you're fast enough."

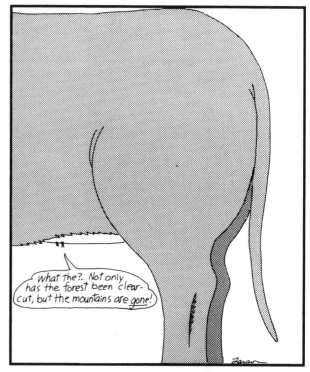

Environmental disasters in a flea's world

The Blob family at home

"My gun, Desmond! I sense this striped man-eater is somewhere dead ahead, waiting to ambush us! Ohhhhhh, he thinks he's so clever."

"Bob! There's a fly on your lip! . . . There he goes. . . .
He's back! He's back!"

Boid watching

Where the deer and the antelope work

In the corridors of Clowngress

"And now the weather — well, doggone it, but I'm afraid that cold front I told you about yesterday is just baaarrreeely going to miss us."

"Come with us, ma'am — and if I were you, I'd get a good lawyer. No one's gonna buy that my-husband-was-only-hibernating story."

Slave-ship entertainers

The class abruptly stopped practicing. Here was an
opportunity to not only employ their skills,
but also to save the entire town.

"Latte, Jed?"

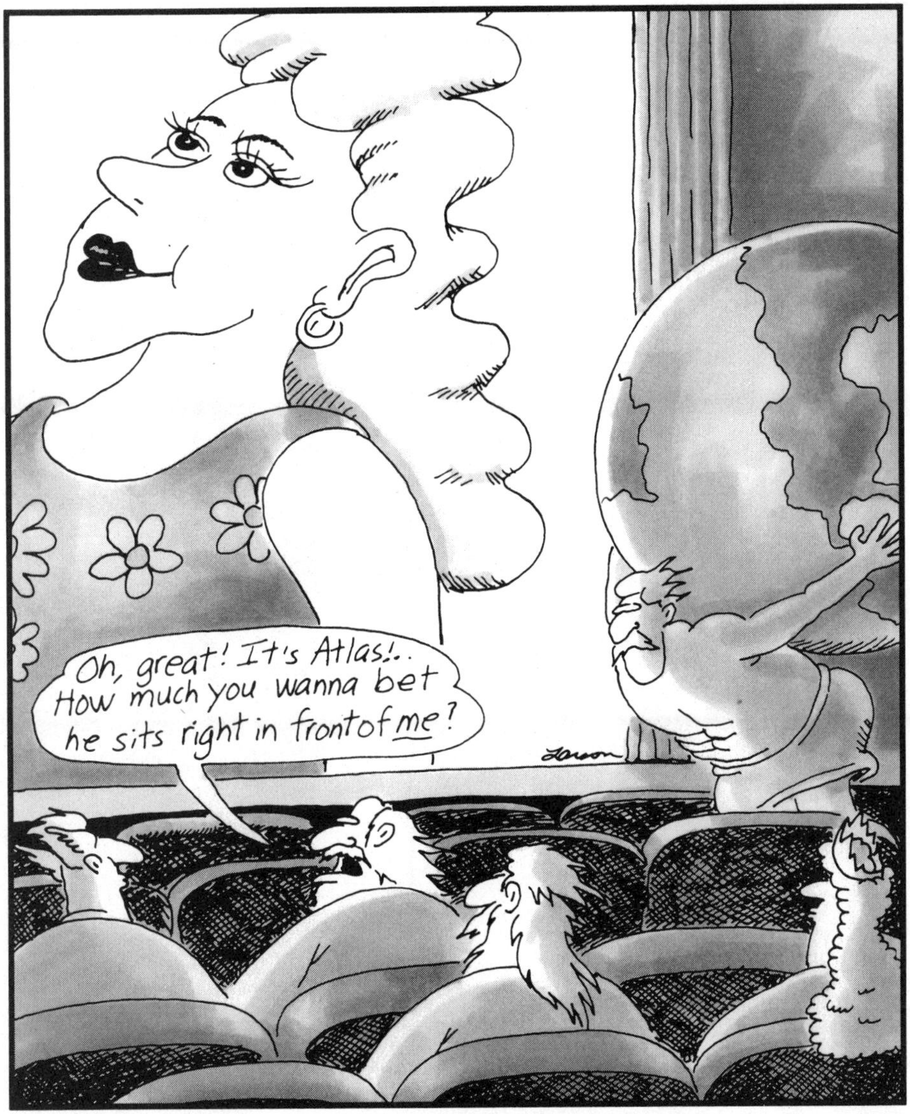
Oh, great! It's Atlas!.. How much you wanna bet he sits right in front of me?

Theater of the Gods

"Oh, yeah? Well, I'd rather be a living corpse made
from dismembered body parts than a
hunchbacked little grave robber like you!"

Giorgio Armani at home

Everything was starting to come into focus for
Farmer MacDougal — his missing sheep, his missing
beer, and his collie, Shep, who was getting just a
little too sociable for his own good.

Early checkers

"I lift, you grab . . . was that concept just a
little too complex, Carl?"

Medieval chicken coops

"Good heavens! Pablo got an 'F' in art! . . . Well, I'm just going to go down to that school myself and meet this teacher face to face!"

Whoa!... Maybe I'll just pass on my usual barking frenzy.

"Oh, this is wonderful, Mr. Gruenfeld — I've only seen it a couple of times. You have corneal corruption. . . . Evil eye, Mr. Gruenfeld, evil eye."

70

While vacationing in Africa, Pinocchio has his longtime wish to be a real boy suddenly and unexpectedly granted.

"Well, I'm not sure if we can afford stomach insurance — right now we're trying to put the kids through the small intestine."

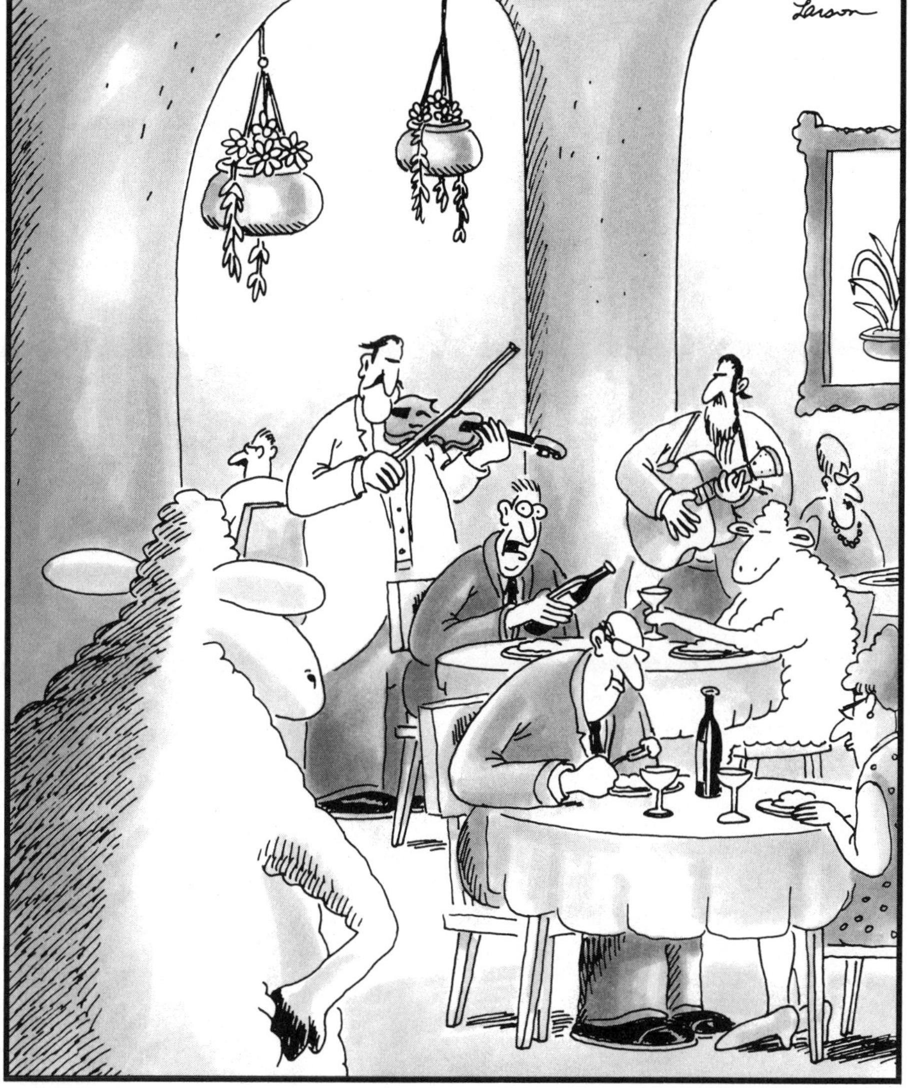
Larson

"Oh my God! It's Yvonne!"

Dance of the Beekeepers

Practical jokes of the Paleolithic

Acts of God

"Well, here we are, my little chickadee."

Alert, but far from panicked, the herbivores studied
the sudden arrival of two cheetah speedwalkers.

"*Lassie! . . Come home! . . . Lassie come home!*"

"OK, crybaby! You want the last soda? Well, let me *get it ready for you!*"

Concepts of hell

"Hey! So I made the wrong decision! . . . But
you know, I really wasn't sure I *wanted* to swing
on a star, carry moonbeams home in a jar!"

Rhino recitals

"Oh, Misty always hates me showing this slide. . . .
It's halftime at the '88 Detroit-Chicago
game when we met."

Clown therapy sessions

"Well, I'll be darned. Says here 70 percent of all accidents happen in the hole."

Where we get calamari blanc

"Eat my apple, will you? *Leave my garden*! *Begone*! . . .
And take all the mole traps with you!"

Scorpion school

Darren was unaware that, under the table, his wife
and Raymond were playing "tentaclies."

"That's why I never walk in front."

"Oh, my word, Helen! You play, *too*? . . . And here I always thought you were just a songbird."

Scene from *Cape Buffalo Fear*

"There you are, my darling . . . Rawlings! Don't move!"

"Oh, yeah? Well, maybe I'll just come
over there and rattle *your* cage!"

God designs the great white shark.

"We don't know exactly who he is, Captain —
a disgruntled worker, we figure."

In Saddam Hussein's war room

Let's see...You make fire--good... You make tools--good...You hunt mammoth...okaaaaaay...Uh-oh! Your references are all baboons--not good.

Primitive resumes

"And here's the jewel of my collection, purchased for a king's ransom from a one-eyed man in Istanbul. . . . I give you Zuzu's petals."

"OK, everyone just stand back! . . . Anyone see what happened here?"

Some of our more common "rescue" animals

"Well, time for our weekly
brain-stem-storming session."

"So please welcome our keynote speaker,
Professor Melvin Fenwick — the man who,
back in 1952, first coined the now common phrase:
'Fools! I'll destroy them all!'"

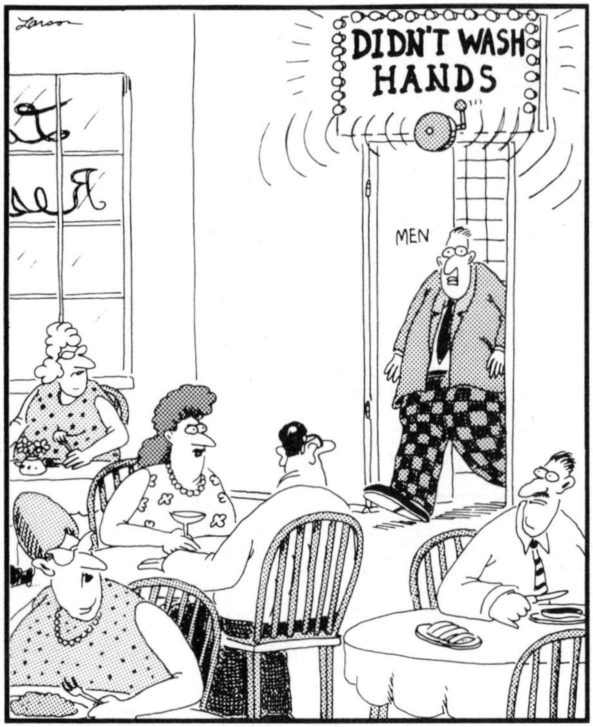
DIDN'T WASH HANDS
MEN

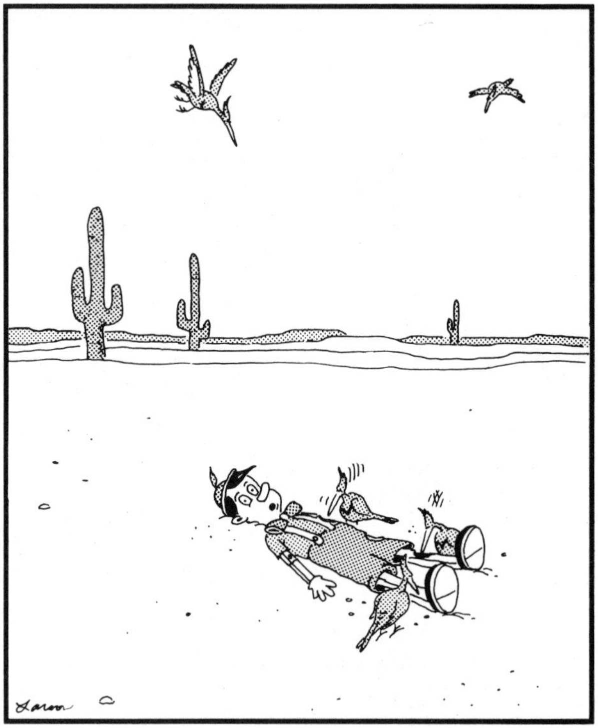

Some wolves, their habitat destroyed and overwhelmed by
human pressures, turn to snorting quack.

"My marriage is in trouble, Barbara. You ever tried communicating with a hammerhead?"

Inside tours of Acme Fake Vomit Inc.